EASY NORDIC
COOKBOOK

77 Scandinavian Recipes for Quick and Tasty Northern Food and Desserts.

By

Adele Tyler

Contents

Introduction

Denmark, Sweden, Finland, Norway, and Iceland are part of the Nordic Region. In the Nordic countries, picking fruit, picking mushrooms, hunting, and fishing are very popular activities, and the first three are readily accessible to foreigners. Almost everywhere there is suitable land for berry picking, and the right of access permits mushroom and such searching.

Fishing is also freely available, although other lure fishing licenses are often easy to obtain. Noma, perhaps the most popular restaurant in the world, was opened in 2003 with the ambition of providing a modern take on the Nordic cuisine. Nordic cuisine has many nutritional benefits, as well.

This book contains many different recipes that you can easily follow with the help of the detailed ingredient list and easy to understand instructions list below each recipe. The recipes contain classic Swedish recipes, classic Norwegian recipes, classic Icelandic recipes, and ancient Viking recipes.

Chapter 1: The World of Classic Swedish Recipes

Following are some classic Swedish recipes that are rich in healthy nutrients and you can easily make them with the detailed instructions list in each recipe:

1.1 Swedish Salmon Burger Recipe

Preparation Time: 30 minutes
Cooking Time: 10 minutes
Serving: 4

Ingredients:

- Fresh chopped dill, three tablespoon
- Salt, to taste
- Black pepper, to taste
- Egg, one
- Capers, one tablespoon
- Bread crumbs, four tablespoon
- Salmon filet, one pound
- Lemon juice, half cup
- Lemon zest, one teaspoon
- Yoghurt, half cup
- Bread buns, four

Instructions:

1. Take a large bowl.
2. Add the eggs, black pepper, capers, salt, and fresh chopped dill.
3. Dip your salmon filet into the egg mixture and then coat the bread crumbs onto the salmon filet.

4. Fry your salmon filet until golden brown on both sides.
5. In a small bowl, add the yoghurt, lemon zest and lemon juice.
6. Make your lemon yoghurt sauce and keep aside.
7. Heat the buns on both sides.
8. Add the salmon filet on the buns.
9. Drop a tablespoon of the yoghurt lemon sauce.
10. Your dish is ready to be served.

1.2 Swedish Potatoes with Dill Cream Sauce Recipe

Preparation Time: 30 minutes
Cooking Time: 10 minutes
Serving: 4

Ingredients:

- Fresh chopped dill, three tablespoon
- Salt, to taste
- Black pepper, to taste
- Butter, two tablespoon
- Flour, one tablespoon
- Milk, one cup
- Russet potatoes, one pound
- Nutmeg, one teaspoon
- Double cream, half cup

Instructions:

1. In a large pan add the butter.
2. Add in the potatoes and fry them in the butter.

3. Add in the milk once the potatoes are cooked properly.
4. Add in the flour, nutmeg and fresh chopped dill.
5. When the milk reduces to half add in the double cream into the mixture.
6. Add the salt and pepper according to your taste.
7. Your dish is ready to be served.

1.3 Swedish Almond and Cardamom Mini Cakes Recipe

Preparation Time: 30 minutes
Cooking Time: 10 minutes
Serving: 4

Ingredients:

- All-purpose flour, one cup
- Sugar, half cup
- Sliced almonds, half cup
- Sea salt, as required
- Baking powder, one tablespoon
- Almond powder, two tablespoon
- Vegetable oil, half cup
- Low fat milk, half cup
- Egg, two
- Vanilla extract, one teaspoon
- Cardamom powder, two tablespoon
- Almond frosting, as required

Instructions:

1. Add the dried ingredients in a large bowl.
2. In a separate bowl, add the low fat milk, vanilla extract, eggs, vegetable oil, and almond powder.
3. Mix the wet ingredients into the dried ingredients.
4. A semi thick mixture is formed.
5. Add the mixture into a muffin tray.
6. Make sure the muffin tray is greased properly.
7. Add in the sliced almonds on top and try to push it into the batter.
8. Bake your mini cakes for ten to fifteen minutes.
9. When the mini cakes are done, dish them out.
10. You can add the almond frosting on top.
11. Your dish is ready to be served.

1.4 Swedish Saffron Buns Recipe

Preparation Time: 30 minutes
Cooking Time: 25 minutes
Serving: 4

Ingredients:

- All-purpose flour, four cups
- Raisins, as required
- Ground cardamom, half teaspoon
- Saffron thread, one teaspoon
- Milk, one cup
- Active yeast, half teaspoon
- Eggs, three
- Sugar, half cup
- Sour cream, a quarter cup

Instructions:

1. In a large bowl, add the active yeast and sugar.
2. In a separate bowl add in the dry ingredients.
3. Add your active yeast mixture into the dry ingredients.
4. Add the sour cream and eggs.
5. Knead your dough and then add in the raisins.
6. Make small buns and place them on a baking tray.
7. Brush the egg mixture on top.
8. Bake your buns for fifteen to twenty minutes.
9. Your dish is ready to be served.

1.5 Swedish Saffron Cake Recipe

Preparation Time: 30 minutes
Cooking Time: 10 minutes
Serving: 4

Ingredients:

- All-purpose flour, one cup
- Sugar, half cup
- Sea salt, as required
- Baking powder, one tablespoon
- Vegetable oil, half cup
- Low fat milk, half cup
- Egg, two
- Vanilla extract, one teaspoon
- Saffron powder, two tablespoon

Instructions:

1. Add the dried ingredients in a large bowl.

2. In a separate bowl, add the low fat milk, vanilla extract, eggs, vegetable oil, and saffron threads.
3. Mix the wet ingredients into the dried ingredients.
4. A semi thick mixture is formed.
5. Add the mixture into a muffin tray.
6. Make sure the muffin tray is greased properly.
7. Bake your mini cakes for ten to fifteen minutes.
8. When the mini cakes are done, dish them out.
9. Your dish is ready to be served.

1.6 Swedish Hash Recipe

Preparation Time: 30 minutes
Cooking Time: 10 minutes
Serving: 4

Ingredients:

- Olive oil, two cups
- Garlic powder, one tablespoon
- Salt to taste
- Pepper to taste
- Red bell pepper, two tablespoon
- Paprika, one tablespoon
- Onion diced, one cup
- Parsley, one tablespoon
- Smoked bacon, one cup
- Diced ham, one cup
- Green pepper, as required

Instructions:

1. Take pan and add olive oil into it.

2. Heat the oil well.
3. Add parsley, garlic powder, paprika and green pepper.
4. Cook them for five minutes.
5. You can add onions now.
6. Cook the mixture again and keep stirring.
7. Add the smoked bacon and diced ham.
8. Continue to cook the ingredients for few minutes.
9. Your dish is ready to serve.

1.7 Swedish Nettle Soup Recipe

Preparation Time: 10 minutes
Cooking Time: 30 minutes
Serving: 4

Ingredients:

- Chopped white onions, one cup
- Chopped blanched nettle leaves, one pound
- Chicken stock, one quart
- Unsalted butter, three tablespoon
- Dried thyme, one teaspoon
- Minced garlic, one teaspoon
- Nutmeg, half teaspoon
- Sour cream, as required
- Lean white fish, one pound

Instructions:

1. In a large pan, add the chopped onions in the butter.
2. When soft and translucent, add in the minced garlic.
3. Add in the stock, thyme, fish, nutmeg and nettles.

4. Add in all the rest of the ingredients and cook the ingredients until the nettles and fish are ready.
5. Blend the soup well.
6. Cook for an extra few minutes.
7. Your dish is ready to be served.

1.8 Swedish Semla Recipe

Preparation Time: 30 minutes
Cooking Time: 10 minutes
Serving: 4

Ingredients:

- Semla dough, two pounds
- Ground almonds, half cup
- Ground cardamom seeds, half teaspoon
- Granulated sugar, a quarter cup
- Vanilla extract, one teaspoon
- Water, three tablespoon
- Vanilla cream, as required
- Egg wash, as required

Instructions:
1. Knead the dough properly.
2. Make small round balls.
3. Place the dough on a baking tray.
4. Apply the egg wash on top of the dough.
5. Bake the Semla balls.
6. When the balls turn golden brown then dish them out.
7. Cut the Semla balls in between.
8. In a bowl mix the rest of ingredients.
9. Add the mixture in between the Semla balls.

10. Your dish is ready to be served.

1.9 Swedish Shrimp Sandwich with Egg, Mayo and Lemon Recipe

Preparation Time: 30 minutes
Cooking Time: 10 minutes
Serving: 4

Ingredients:

- Mayonnaise, two tablespoon
- Salad leaves, as required
- Cooked shrimps, half pound
- Lemon juice, three tablespoon
- Fried eggs, as required
- Fresh chopped dill, one tablespoon
- Bread slices, as required
- Sugar, one tablespoon

Instructions:

1. In a bowl, mix the mayonnaise, lemon juice and sugar until it forms a homogenous mixture.
2. Toast your bread slices.
3. Add the mayonnaise, lemon juice and sugar mixture on top of the slices.
4. Add the cooked shrimps.
5. Layer the fried eggs and then the fresh chopped dill on top.
6. Add the salad leaves.
7. Your dish is ready to be served.

1.10 Swedish Hasselback Potatoes Recipe

Preparation Time: 30 minutes
Cooking Time: 10 minutes
Serving: 4

Ingredients:

- Fresh chopped dill, three tablespoon
- Salt, to taste
- Black pepper, to taste
- Mozzarella cheese, one cup
- Capers, one tablespoon
- Lemon juice, half cup
- Sour cream, as required
- Chopped parsley, half cup

Instructions:

1. Wash your potatoes.
2. Cut the potatoes in such a way that they are not separated fully but are attached at the end.
3. In a small bowl, add the sour cream, lemon juice, chopped parsley, capers, salt and pepper.
4. Add the formed mixture above onto the potatoes making sure that the mixture reaches to each part of the potatoes.
5. Lay your potatoes on a baking tray.
6. Add the mozzarella cheese on top.
7. Bake your potatoes.
8. Add the fresh chopped dill on top.
9. Your dish is ready to be served.

1.11 Swedish Egg Salad with Anchovies Recipe

Preparation Time: 30 minutes
Cooking Time: 10 minutes
Serving: 4

Ingredients:

- Fresh chopped dill, three tablespoon
- Salt, to taste
- Black pepper, to taste
- Eggs, four
- Capers, one tablespoon
- Diced anchovies, four tablespoon
- Lemon juice, half cup
- Lemon zest, one teaspoon
- Sour cream, half cup

Instructions:

1. Boil your eggs in salted water.
2. Peel your eggs and slice them up.
3. In a large bowl add the salt, pepper, lemon zest, lemon juice, capers and sour cream.
4. Mix your ingredients well to form a homogenized mixture.
5. Add the boiled eggs and diced anchovies in a bowl.
6. Pour the formed mixture on top and mix it.
7. Add the chopped dill on top.
8. Your dish is ready to be served.

1.12 Swedish Sausage and Macaroni Recipe

Preparation Time: 30 minutes
Cooking Time: 10 minutes
Serving: 4

Ingredients:

- Fresh chopped dill, three tablespoon
- Salt, to taste
- Black pepper, to taste
- Macaroni, one pack
- Minced garlic, one teaspoon
- Chopped onion, one cup
- Butter, two tablespoon
- Capers, one tablespoon
- Chicken sausage, one pound
- Lemon juice, half cup
- Mozzarella cheese, one cup
- Sour cream, half cup

Instructions:

1. In a large pan, add the butter.
2. Add in the chopped onions.
3. When the onions are soft enough, add the minced garlic.
4. Cook your onions and then add the sausages.
5. Add in the salt, pepper, lemon juice and capers.
6. Cook your sausages properly.
7. Boil your macaroni and drain it.
8. Add in the macaroni, sour cream and mozzarella cheese into the pan.
9. Cook your dish until the cheese melts.
10. Your dish is ready to be served.

1.13 Swedish Toast Skagen Recipe

Preparation Time: 30 minutes
Cooking Time: 10 minutes
Serving: 4

Ingredients:

- Fresh chopped dill, three tablespoon
- Salt, to taste
- Black pepper, to taste
- Mayonnaise, half cup
- Capers, one tablespoon
- Crème fraiche, three tablespoon
- Cooked shrimps, one pound
- Lemon juice, half cup
- Lemon zest, one teaspoon
- Golden white fish caviar, for garnishing
- Bread slices, as required

Instructions:

1. In a large bowl, add the mayonnaise, salt, black pepper, lemon juice, lemon zest, capers, crème fraiche and cooked shrimps.
2. Mix all the ingredients and then set aside.
3. In a pan, add the butter and toast your bread slices.
4. Add the formed mixture on top of each toast.
5. Add the golden white fish caviar on top.
6. Garnish it with chopped fresh dill.
7. Your dish is ready to be served.

1.14 Swedish Beef Ryeberg Recipe

Preparation Time: 10 minutes
Cooking Time: 25 minutes
Serving: 4

Ingredients:

- Fresh chopped dill, three tablespoon
- Salt, to taste
- Black pepper, to taste
- Butter, four tablespoon
- Beef, one pound
- Worcestershire sauce, four tablespoon
- Potatoes, one pound
- Chopped onions, half cup
- Parsley, for garnishing

Instructions:

1. In a large pan add the butter and chopped onions.
2. Cook your onions until they turn translucent.
3. Add in the beef and potatoes.
4. Add the salt, pepper and Worcestershire sauce to taste.
5. Cover your dish and cook it for fifteen minutes.
6. Add chopped parsleys on top.
7. Your dish is ready to be served.

1.15 Swedish Small Potato Pancakes Recipe

Preparation Time: 10 minutes
Cooking Time: 5 minutes
Serving: 2

Ingredients:

- Fresh chopped dill, half cup
- Eggs, three
- Baking powder, one tablespoon
- Cooking oil, one tablespoon
- All-purpose flour, half cup
- Milk, half cup
- Vanilla extract, one teaspoon
- Small potatoes, half cup

Instructions:

1. In a large bowl, add in the eggs.
2. Mix the eggs until a smooth mixture is formed.
3. Add in the rest of the ingredients one by one ensuring not to form any clusters.
4. Add in the potatoes in the end.
5. Add cooking oil in a pan.
6. Add some amount of the pancake mix into the pan and cook effectively.
7. Cook your pan cakes on both sides until it turns golden brown.
8. Your dish is ready to be served.

1.16 Swedish Poached Salmon Recipe

Preparation Time: 10 minutes
Cooking Time: 30 minutes
Serving: 2

Ingredients:

- Salmon cubes, half pound
- Ground ginger, a quarter teaspoon
- Pecan pieces, two tablespoon
- Tomato paste, one cup
- Pepper, as required
- Red chili powder, one teaspoon
- Cilantro, half cup
- Salt, a quarter teaspoon
- Red chili paste, one tablespoon
- Sour cream, as required

Instructions:

1. Boil the salmon cubes.
2. In a large pan, add all the ingredients except the salmon pieces.
3. Cook your tomato sauce.
4. Add the salmon pieces and let them simmer for five to ten minutes.
5. Add the sour cream on top.
6. Your dish is ready to be served.

1.17 Swedish Rhubarb Compote Recipe

Preparation Time: 10 minutes
Cooking Time: 20 minutes
Serving: 4

Ingredients:

- Turbinado sugar, three tablespoon
- Whipping cream, as required
- Rhubarb, one and a half pounds
- Cornstarch, two tablespoon
- Sugar, one cup
- Vanilla extract, one teaspoon
- Brown sugar, two tablespoon
- Water, one cup

Instructions:

1. In a large sauce pan, add the water.
2. Add the sugar and rhubarb.
3. Boil your rhubarb well.
4. Add the vanilla extract and cornstarch.
5. Cook your compote until your mixture starts to thicken.
6. Dish out your compote.
7. Mix the whipping cream and brown sugar.
8. Add the whipped cream on top of the compote.
9. Your dish is ready to be served.

1.18 Swedish Sandwich Cake Recipe

Preparation Time: 30 minutes
Cooking Time: 10 minutes
Serving: 4

Ingredients:

- Fresh chopped dill, three tablespoon
- Salt, to taste
- Black pepper, to taste
- English bread, as required
- Butter, one tablespoon
- Cucumber slices, as required
- Salmon filet, one pound
- Mayonnaise, half cup
- Cooked prawns, half pound
- Hard boiled eggs, as required

Instructions:

1. Take the English bread and take it on a dish.
2. Spread the mayonnaise on top of the bread.
3. Layer the salmon filet, cooked prawns and then the hard boiled eggs.
4. Add the butter on top and then the cucumber slices.
5. Add salt and pepper on top and roll your sandwich.
6. Add fresh chopped dill on top.
7. Slice your sandwich.
8. Your dish is ready to be served.

1.19 Swedish Spinach Soup Recipe

Preparation Time: 10 minutes
Cooking Time: 10 minutes
Serving: 4

Ingredients:

- Chopped white onions, one cup
- Chopped blanched spinach leaves, one pound
- Chicken stock, one quart
- Unsalted butter, three tablespoon
- Dried thyme, one teaspoon
- Minced garlic, one teaspoon
- Nutmeg, half teaspoon
- Sour cream, as required
- Lean white fish, one pound

Instructions:

1. In a large pan, add the chopped onions in the butter.
2. When soft and translucent, add in the minced garlic.
3. Add in the stock, thyme, fish, nutmeg and the spinach leaves.
4. Add in all the rest of the ingredients and cook the ingredients until the spinach and fish are ready.
5. Blend the soup well.
6. Cook your soup for an extra few minutes.
7. Your dish is ready to be served.

1.20 Swedish Split-Pea Soup with Bacon Recipe

Preparation Time: 10 minutes
Cooking Time: 10 minutes
Serving: 4

Ingredients:

- Chopped white onions, one cup
- Chopped blanched pea, one pound
- Chicken stock, one quart
- Unsalted butter, three tablespoon
- Dried thyme, one teaspoon
- Minced garlic, one teaspoon
- Nutmeg, half teaspoon
- Sour cream, as required
- Lean chopped bacon, one pound

Instructions:

1. In a large pan, add the chopped onions in the butter.
2. When soft and translucent, add in the minced garlic.
3. Add in the stock, thyme, nutmeg and the split peas.
4. Add in all the rest of the ingredients and cook the ingredients until the split pea is ready.
5. Blend the soup well.
6. Cook your soup for an extra few minutes.
7. Cook your chopped bacon pieces.
8. Add your soup in a serving bowl.

9. Crumble your bacon slices and add the bacon crumble on top of your soup.
8. You can also garnish it with chopped fresh dill.
9. Your dish is ready to be served.

Chapter 2: The World of Classic Norwegian Recipes

Following are some classic Norwegian recipes that are rich in healthy nutrients and you can easily make them with the detailed instructions list in each recipe:

2.1 Norwegian Meatballs Recipe

Preparation Time: 30 minutes
Cooking Time: 10 minutes
Serving: 4

Ingredients:

- Eggs, two
- Salt, to taste
- Black pepper, to taste
- Milk, one cup
- Onion, one cup
- Bread crumbs, one cup
- Sugar, two tablespoon
- Minced pork meat, one pound
- Beef stock, three cup
- Minced beef meat, one pound
- Minced ginger, two tablespoon
- Cayenne pepper, a dash
- Butter, two tablespoon
- All-purpose flour, five tablespoon
- Heavy whipping cream, one cup

Instructions:

1. Take a large bowl.
2. Add the oil and onions into the bowl.

3. Add the chopped ginger into the bowl.
4. Add the minced beef, and minced pork into the bowl.
5. Add the spices, eggs and bread crumbs.
6. Mix all the ingredients together.
7. Shape your beef and pork mixture into round meatballs.
8. Heat a grilling pan.
9. Add the olive oil on top.
10. Place the meatballs on top.
11. Fry your meatballs on both sides until they turn golden brown.
12. Fry all the meatballs and dish them out.
13. In a large pan, add the rest of the ingredients.
14. Add the meatballs into the mixture.
15. Cook your meatballs until dried.
16. Your dish is ready to be served.

2.2 Norwegian Gravlax Recipe

Preparation Time: 30 minutes
Cooking Time: 10 minutes
Serving: 4

Ingredients:

- Fresh chopped dill, three tablespoon
- Salt, to taste
- Black pepper, to taste
- Granulated white sugar, two tablespoon
- Salmon filet, one pound
- Egg yolks, four

- Olive oil, a quarter cup
- White sugar, one tablespoon
- Mustard, one tablespoon
- White vinegar, one tablespoon
- White pepper, one tablespoon

Instructions:

1. In a large pan, prepare the gravlax sauce.
2. Add in the white sugar, olive oil, egg yolks, mustard, white vinegar and white pepper.
3. Place the pan on low heat and mix the sauce until it is homogenized in mixture.
4. When the sauce is cooked, pour it into a small bowl.
5. Add the rest of the ingredients onto the salmon filet.
6. Let your salmon marinate for a couple of hours.
7. Slice your salmon.
8. Pour the gravlax sauce onto the salmon slices.
9. Your dish is ready to be served.

2.3 Norwegian Ribbe Recipe

Preparation Time: 30 minutes
Cooking Time: 10 minutes
Serving: 4

Ingredients:

- Fresh chopped dill, three tablespoon
- Salt, to taste
- Black pepper, to taste
- Water, half cup
- Capers, one tablespoon

- Caraway seeds, four tablespoon
- Pork ribs, one pound
- Green cabbage, half cup
- Bacon slice, as required
- Olive oil, as required

Instructions:

1. In a large bowl, add the pork ribs, caraway seeds, capers, salt and black pepper.
2. Mix all the ingredients together and add the water into it.
3. Cook your pork ribs well.
4. Cook your bacon slices and then dish them out.
5. Cook your shredded cabbage and stir-fry.
6. In a plate serve your ribs with the stir-fried cabbage and crumble your bacon slices on top.
7. Your dish is ready to be served.

2.4 Norwegian Klubb Dumplings Recipe

Preparation Time: 30 minutes
Cooking Time: 20 minutes
Serving: 4

Ingredients:

- Baking powder, a quarter teaspoon
- Cooked ham, half pound
- All-purpose flour, two cups
- Ground black pepper, as required
- Salt, as required
- Potatoes, four cups
- Melted butter, one cup

Instructions:

1. Add the baking powder, all-purpose flour, salt and ground black pepper into a bowl and mix it.
2. Peel your potatoes and mash them.
3. Add the potato mixture into the flour mixture and mix properly.
4. Add the melted butter into the mixture.
5. Form a dough from the mixture formed above.
6. Add the slices of ham into the formed dough and make small round balls.
7. In a large pan full of boiling water, add the balls and cook them.
8. Your dish is ready to be served.

2.5 Norwegian Steamed Salmon Recipe

Preparation Time: 10 minutes
Cooking Time: 15 minutes
Serving: 2

Ingredients:

- Bok choy, two
- Lemons, two
- Fresh basil, one cup
- Olive oil, a quarter cup
- Salmon filet, one pound
- Balsamic vinegar, four tablespoon

Instructions:

1. Take a large bowl.
2. Add in all the ingredients and mix them well.
3. Cook your salmon filet by steaming.

4. You can steam your salmon filet in a pan or any other dish.
5. When cooked, you can serve them with any side dish you want.
6. Your dish is ready to be served.

2.6 Norwegian Fish Cakes Recipe

Preparation Time: 30 minutes
Cooking Time: 10 minutes
Serving: 4

Ingredients:

- Hake fillet, one pound
- Heavy cream, one cup
- Unsalted butter, six tablespoon
- Distilled white vinegar, one tablespoon
- Chili powder, half tablespoon
- Olive oil, one cup
- Fresh chopped dill, one tablespoon
- Mayonnaise, one cup
- Salt to taste
- Pepper to taste

Instructions:

1. Mince your hake filet.
2. In a large bowl, add your minced hake, distilled white vinegar, chili powder, olive oil, salt and pepper.
3. Mix everything properly and make small fish cakes out of it.
4. Cook your fish cakes in the unsalted butter until they become golden brown in color.

5. When done, dish them out.
6. In a small bowl, mix the rest of the ingredients and serve your fish cakes with the formed sauce.
7. Your dish is ready to be served.

2.7 Norwegian Lamb and Cabbage Recipe

Preparation Time: 30 minutes
Cooking Time: 10 minutes
Serving: 4

Ingredients:

- Fresh chopped dill, three tablespoon
- Salt, to taste
- Black pepper, to taste
- Capers, one tablespoon
- All-purpose flour, one tablespoon
- Lamb cubes, one pound
- Lemon juice, half cup
- Lemon zest, one teaspoon
- Cabbage, two cups
- Olive oil, two tablespoon
- Water, two cups

Instructions:

1. In a large pan, add the olive oil and heat it.
2. Add in the lamb cubes.
3. Cook your lamb cubes by adding salt and pepper into it.
4. Add the lemon juice and lemon zest into the lamb cubes.
5. Add the cappers, cabbage and water once the lamb cubes are half cooked.

6. Once everything is cooked, add the all-purpose flour and mix it.
7. Boil your dish and then garnish it with chopped fresh dill.
8. Your dish is ready to be served.

2.8 Norwegian Cod and Potatoes Recipe

Preparation Time: 30 minutes
Cooking Time: 10 minutes
Serving: 4

Ingredients:

- Fresh chopped dill, three tablespoon
- Salt, to taste
- Black pepper, to taste
- Capers, one tablespoon
- All-purpose flour, one tablespoon
- Cod cubes, one pound
- Lemon juice, half cup
- Lemon zest, one teaspoon
- Potatoes, two cups
- Olive oil, two tablespoon
- Water, two cups

Instructions:

1. In a large pan, add the olive oil and heat it.
2. Add in the cod cubes.
3. Cook your cod cubes by adding salt and pepper into it.
4. Add the lemon juice and lemon zest into the cod cubes.

5. Add the cappers, potatoes and water once the cod cubes are half cooked.
6. Once everything is cooked, add the all-purpose flour and mix it.
7. Boil your dish and then garnish it with chopped fresh dill.
8. Your dish is ready to be served.

2.9 Norwegian Meatballs with Gravy Recipe

Preparation Time: 30 minutes
Cooking Time: 10 minutes
Serving: 4

Ingredients:

- Eggs, two
- Salt, to taste
- Black pepper, to taste
- Milk, one cup
- Onion, one cup
- Bread crumbs, one cup
- Sugar, two tablespoon
- Minced pork meat, one pound
- Beef stock, three cup
- Minced beef meat, one pound
- Minced ginger, two tablespoon
- Cayenne pepper, a dash
- Butter, two tablespoon
- All-purpose flour, five tablespoon
- Tomato paste, one cup

Instructions:

1. Take a large bowl.
2. Add the oil and onions into the bowl.
3. Add the chopped ginger into the bowl.
4. Add the minced beef, and minced pork into the bowl.
5. Add the spices, eggs and bread crumbs.
6. Mix all the ingredients together.
7. Shape your beef and pork mixture into round meatballs.
8. Heat a grilling pan.
9. Add the olive oil on top.
10. Place the meatballs on top.
11. Fry your meatballs on both sides until they turn golden brown.
12. Fry all the meatballs and dish them out.
13. In a large pan, add the rest of the ingredients.
14. Add the meatballs into the mixture.
15. Cook the meatballs for ten minutes.
16. Your dish is ready to be served.

2.10 Norwegian Salmon with Matcha Spice Recipe

Preparation Time: 10 minutes
Cooking Time: 15 minutes
Serving: 2

Ingredients:

- Bok choy, two
- Lemons, two
- Fresh basil, one cup

- Olive oil, a quarter cup
- Salmon filet, one pound
- Balsamic vinegar, four tablespoon
- Matcha spice, two teaspoon
- White vinegar, half cup
- Salt, as required
- Black pepper, as required

Instructions:

1. Take a large bowl.
2. Add in all the ingredients and mix them well.
3. Cook your salmon filet by steaming.
4. You can steam your salmon filet in a pan or any other dish.
5. When cooked, dish it out.
6. Add the rest of the ingredients into a bowl and cook your matcha mixture.
7. When cooked, pour it onto your salmon filet.
8. Your dish is ready to be served.

2.11 Norwegian Fish and Root Vegetable Chowder Recipe

Preparation Time: 15 minutes
Cooking Time: 20 minutes
Serving: 4

Ingredients:

- Fish broth, one cup
- Onion, one cup
- Heavy cream, one cup
- Fish mince, half pound
- Powdered cumin, half tablespoon

- Smoked paprika, half teaspoon
- Water, one cup
- Root vegetables, one cup
- Minced garlic, two tablespoon
- Minced ginger, two tablespoon
- Cilantro, half cup
- Olive oil, two tablespoon
- Chopped tomatoes, one cup

Instructions:

1. Take a pan.
2. Add in the oil and onions.
3. Cook the onions until they become soft and fragrant.
4. Add in the chopped garlic and ginger.
5. Cook the mixture and add the tomatoes into it.
6. Add the spices and fish mince.
7. Add in the broth.
8. Add in the root vegetables.
9. Mix the ingredients carefully and cover your pan.
10. Add cilantro on top.
11. You can serve with chopped dill on top.
12. Your dish is ready to be served.

2.12 Norwegian Betasuppe Recipe

Preparation Time: 10 minutes
Cooking Time: 10 minutes
Serving: 4

Ingredients:

- Chopped white onions, one cup
- Chopped blanched pea, one pound

- Chicken stock, one quart
- Unsalted butter, three tablespoon
- Dried thyme, one teaspoon
- Minced garlic, one teaspoon
- Nutmeg, half teaspoon
- Celery root, two cups
- Leeks, two cups
- Lean chopped bacon, one pound

Instructions:

1. In a large pan, add the chopped onions in the butter.
2. When soft and translucent, add in the minced garlic.
3. Add in the stock, thyme, nutmeg and the split peas.
4. Add in all the rest of the ingredients and cook the ingredients until the split pea is ready.
5. Blend the soup well.
6. Cook your soup for an extra few minutes.
7. Cook your chopped bacon pieces.
8. Add your soup in a serving bowl.
9. Crumble your bacon slices and add the bacon crumble on top of your soup.
10. You can also garnish it with chopped fresh dill.
11. Your dish is ready to be served.

2.13 Norwegian Beef Stew Recipe

Preparation Time: 10 minutes
Cooking Time: 40 minutes
Serving: 2

Ingredients:

- Beef broth, one cup
- Turmeric powder, one teaspoon
- Onion, one cup
- Lemon juice, half cup
- Beef mince, half pound
- Powdered cumin, half tablespoon
- Smoked paprika, half teaspoon
- Water, one cup
- Minced garlic, two tablespoon
- Minced ginger, two tablespoon
- Cilantro, half cup
- Olive oil, two tablespoon
- Chopped tomatoes, one cup

Instructions:

1. Take a pan.
2. Add in the oil and onions.
3. Cook the onions until they become soft and fragrant.
4. Add in the chopped garlic and ginger.
5. Cook the mixture and add the tomatoes into it.
6. Add the spices and beef mince.
7. Add in the broth.
8. Mix the ingredients carefully and cover your pan.

9. Add cilantro on top.
10. Your dish is ready to be served.

2.14 Norwegian Steak Recipe

Preparation Time: 20 minutes
Cooking Time: 10 minutes
Serving: 4

Ingredients:

- Fresh chopped dill, three tablespoon
- Salt, to taste
- Black pepper, to taste
- Lemon spice mix, two tablespoon
- Capers, one tablespoon
- Beef steak, one and a half pound
- Horseradish, one teaspoon
- Dry white wine, half cup
- Olive oil, one tablespoon

Instructions:

1. In a large bowl, add all the ingredients.
2. Mix everything properly and make sure the beef steak is coated with the marinade properly.
3. Preheat an oven.
4. Lay your beef steak on a baking tray.
5. Make sure your baking dish is greased properly.
6. Roast your beef steak for ten to fifteen minutes.
7. Slice it up and serve it on a side with roasted vegetables if you like.
8. Your dish is ready to be served.

2.15 Norwegian Burgers with Mushroom Sauce Recipe

Preparation Time: 30 minutes
Cooking Time: 10 minutes
Serving: 4

Ingredients:

- Fresh chopped dill, three tablespoon
- Salt, to taste
- Black pepper, to taste
- Egg, one
- Capers, one tablespoon
- Bread crumbs, four tablespoon
- Beef filet, one pound
- Mayonnaise, half cup
- Fresh dill, one teaspoon
- Mushrooms, one cup
- Bread buns, four

Instructions:

1. Take a large bowl.
2. Add the eggs, black pepper, capers, salt, and fresh chopped dill.
3. Dip your beef filet into the egg mixture and then coat the bread crumbs onto the beef filet.
4. Fry your beef filet until golden brown on both sides.
5. In a small bowl, add the mushrooms, mayonnaise and chopped dill.
6. Make your mushroom sauce and keep aside.
7. Heat the buns on both sides.

8. Add the beef filet on the buns.
9. Drop a tablespoon of the mushroom sauce.
10. Your dish is ready to be served.

2.16 Norwegian Smoked Salmon Quiche Recipe

Preparation Time: 30 minutes
Cooking Time: 10 minutes
Serving: 4

Ingredients:

- Smoked salmon, half pound
- Turmeric powder, one teaspoon
- Onion, one cup
- Smoked paprika, half teaspoon
- Minced garlic, two tablespoon
- Minced ginger, two tablespoon
- Olive oil, two tablespoon
- Eggs, two
- Milk, half cup
- Quiche dough, as required
- Corn, one cup
- Chopped tomatoes, one cup

Instructions:

1. Take a pan.
2. Add in the oil and onions.
3. Cook the onions until they become soft and fragrant.
4. Add in the chopped garlic and ginger.
5. Cook the mixture and add the tomatoes into it.
6. Add the spices.

7. When the tomatoes are done, add the smoked salmon into it.
8. Mix the ingredients carefully and cover your pan.
9. When the smoked salmon, add the eggs and milk into it.
10. Lay your dough in a baking dish and pour the quiche mixture on top.
11. Bake your quiche for twenty minutes.
12. When done, dish it out.
13. Your dish is ready to be served.

2.17 Norwegian Stuffed Potato Patties Recipe

Preparation Time: 25 minutes
Cooking Time: 15 minutes
Serving: 4

Ingredients:

- Chopped garlic, two teaspoon
- Green onions, three tablespoon
- Bread crumbs, half cup
- Bacon meat, two cups
- Chopped fresh dill, two tablespoon
- Vegetable oil, two tablespoon
- Salt to taste
- Cooked potatoes, two cups
- Black pepper to taste
- Eggs, two
- Chopped onions, two tablespoon

Instructions:

1. In a large bowl, add in the onions and the garlic.
2. Add in the rest of the ingredients.
3. Make round patties from the mixture.
4. Add the bacon meat in the middle and cover your potato patties all over.
5. In a pan, heat the vegetable oil.
6. Fry your stuffed potato patties.
7. Dish your patties out when the patties turn golden brown on both sides.
8. Add cilantro on top.
9. You can serve it with any sauce that you prefer.
10. Your dish is ready to be served.

2.18 Norwegian Cauliflower with Shrimp Sauce Recipe

Preparation Time: 20 minutes
Cooking Time: 10 minutes
Serving: 4

Ingredients:

- Fresh chopped dill, three tablespoon
- Salt, to taste
- Black pepper, to taste
- Lemon spice mix, two tablespoon
- Capers, one tablespoon
- Cauliflower, one and a half pound
- Horseradish, one teaspoon
- Shrimps, one cup
- Heavy cream, one cup
- Mayonnaise, two tablespoon
- Dry white wine, half cup
- Olive oil, one tablespoon

Instructions:

1. In a large bowl, add all the ingredients.
2. Mix everything properly and make sure the cauliflower is coated with the marinade properly.
3. Preheat the oven.
4. Lay your cauliflower on a baking tray.
5. Make sure your baking dish is properly greased.
6. Roast your cauliflower for ten to fifteen minutes.
7. In a saucepan, add the dry wine, mayonnaise, heavy cream and shrimp.
8. Cook it and then grind it.
9. Pour your sauce over your roasted vegetables.
10. Your dish is ready to be served.

2.19 Norwegian Lemon Chicken Skillet Recipe

Preparation Time: 10 minutes
Cooking Time: 30 minutes
Serving: 4

Ingredients:

- Powdered cumin, one tablespoon
- Salt, to taste
- Black pepper, to taste
- Turmeric powder, one teaspoon
- Onion, one cup
- Chicken broth, one cup
- Smoked paprika, half teaspoon
- Water, half cup
- Chicken breast, one pound
- Minced garlic, two tablespoon

- Minced ginger, two tablespoon
- Cilantro, half cup
- Olive oil, two tablespoon
- Chopped tomatoes, one cup
- Lemon juice, one cup

Instructions:

1. Take a pan.
2. Add in the oil and onions.
3. Cook the onions until they become soft and fragrant.
4. Add in the chopped garlic and ginger.
5. Cook the mixture and add the tomatoes into it.
6. Add the spices.
7. When the tomatoes are done, add the chicken into it.
8. Mix the chicken so that the tomatoes and spices are coated all over the chicken.
9. Cook for five minutes.
10. Add in the water and lemon juice.
11. Mix the ingredients carefully and cover your pan.
12. When your chicken is done, add in the cilantro.
13. Mix your chicken and let it cook for an additional five minutes.
14. Your dish is ready to be served.

2.20 Norwegian Poached Salmon with Anchovy Butter Recipe

Preparation Time: 10 minutes
Cooking Time: 30 minutes
Serving: 2

Ingredients:

- Salmon cubes, half pound
- Ground ginger, a quarter teaspoon
- Anchovy butter, two tablespoon
- Pepper, as required
- Red chili powder, one teaspoon
- Cilantro, half cup
- Salt, a quarter teaspoon
- Red chili paste, one tablespoon
- Sour cream, as required

Instructions:

1. Boil the salmon cubes.
2. In a large pan, add all the ingredients except the salmon pieces.
3. Cook your anchovy butter.
4. Add the salmon pieces and let them simmer for five to ten minutes.
5. Add the sour cream on top.
6. Your dish is ready to be served.

Chapter 3: The World of Classic Icelandic Recipes

Following are some classic Icelandic recipes that are rich in healthy nutrients and you can easily make them with the detailed instructions list in each recipe:

3.1 Icelandic Fish Soup Recipe

Preparation Time: 10 minutes
Cooking Time: 20 minutes
Serving: 4

Ingredients:

- Chopped white onions, one cup
- Chopped celery, one pound
- Potatoes, one cup
- Chicken stock, one quart
- Unsalted butter, three tablespoon
- Dried thyme, one teaspoon
- Minced garlic, one teaspoon
- Nutmeg, half teaspoon
- Heavy cream, one cup
- Tomato paste, one cup
- Lean white fish, one pound

Instructions:

1. In a large pan, add the chopped onions in the butter.
2. When soft and translucent, add in the minced garlic.

3. Add in the stock, thyme, fish, nutmeg, potatoes and the celery leaves.
4. Add in all the rest of the ingredients and cook the ingredients until the celery and potatoes are ready.
5. Cook the soup well for ten minutes and then check you soup.
6. If not thick the cook your soup for an extra few minutes.
7. Your dish is ready to be served.

3.2 Icelandic Lamb Soup Recipe

Preparation Time: 10 minutes
Cooking Time: 10 minutes
Serving: 4

Ingredients:

- Chopped white onions, one cup
- Chopped celery, one pound
- Potatoes, one cup
- Chicken stock, one quart
- Unsalted butter, three tablespoon
- Dried thyme, one teaspoon
- Minced garlic, one teaspoon
- Nutmeg, half teaspoon
- Heavy cream, one cup
- Tomato paste, one cup
- Lamb meat one pound

Instructions:

1. In a large pan, add the chopped onions in the butter.
2. When soft and translucent, add in the minced garlic.
3. Add in the stock, thyme, lamb, nutmeg, potatoes and the celery leaves.
4. Add in all the rest of the ingredients and cook the ingredients until the lamb and potatoes are ready.
5. Cook the soup well for ten minutes and then check you soup.
6. If not thick, the cook your soup for an extra few minutes.
7. Your dish is ready to be served.

3.3 Icelandic Breaded Lamb Loin Chops Recipe

Preparation Time: 30 minutes
Cooking Time: 10 minutes
Serving: 4

Ingredients:

- Fresh chopped dill, three tablespoon
- Salt, to taste
- Black pepper, to taste
- Egg, one
- Capers, one tablespoon
- Bread crumbs, four tablespoon
- Lamb chops, one pound
- Lemon juice, half cup
- Lemon zest, one teaspoon
- Yoghurt, half cup

Instructions:

1. Take a large bowl.
2. Add the eggs, black pepper, capers, salt, and fresh chopped dill.
3. Dip your lamb chops into the egg mixture and then coat the bread crumbs onto the lamb chops.
4. Fry your lamb chops until golden brown on both sides.
5. In a small bowl, add the yoghurt, lemon zest and lemon juice.
6. Make your lemon yoghurt sauce and keep aside.
7. Drop a tablespoon of the yoghurt lemon sauce.
8. Your dish is ready to be served.

3.4 Icelandic Pickled Beets Recipe

Preparation Time: 30 minutes
Cooking Time: 10 minutes
Serving: 4

Ingredients:

- Brown sugar, half cup
- Prepared beets, five cups
- Pickle spice, one and a half tablespoon
- White vinegar, one cup
- Water, three cups

Instructions:

1. Heat a sauce pan.
2. Add the water and boil it.

3. Add the brown sugar and boil the mixture.
4. When the sugar melts, add the white vinegar and prepared beets.
5. Add the pickle spice and cook the mixture.
6. Add your mixture into a jar.
7. Cool your mixture completely.
8. Close the lid of your jar and refrigerate.
9. Your dish is ready to be served.

3.5 Icelandic Guacamole Nachos Recipe

Preparation Time: 30 minutes
Cooking Time: 10 minutes
Serving: 4

Ingredients:

- Fresh chopped dill, three tablespoon
- Salt, to taste
- Black pepper, to taste
- Nachos, one pack
- Avocado, one
- Grained cheese, one pound
- Salsa, one cup

Instructions:

1. Cut the avocado and make a paste.
2. Add the nachos in a baking dish.
3. Add the cheese, salt and pepper on top.
4. Melt the cheese and then add the salsa and guacamole on top.
5. Add the fresh chopped dill to garnish.
6. Your dish is ready to be served.

3.6 Icelandic Cod with Avocado and Chorizo Recipe

Preparation Time: 30 minutes
Cooking Time: 10 minutes
Serving: 4

Ingredients:

- Fresh chopped dill, three tablespoon
- Salt, to taste
- Black pepper, to taste
- Capers, one tablespoon
- All-purpose flour, one tablespoon
- Cod cubes, one pound
- Lemon juice, half cup
- Lemon zest, one teaspoon
- Chorizo, two cups
- Olive oil, two tablespoon
- Avocado, two
- Water, two cups

Instructions:

1. In a large pan, add the olive oil and heat it.
2. Add in the cod cubes.
3. Cook your cod cubes by adding salt and pepper into it.
4. Add the lemon juice and lemon zest into the cod cubes.
5. Add the cappers, chorizo and water once the cod cubes are half cooked.

6. Once everything is cooked add the all-purpose flour and mix it.
7. Boil your dish and then garnish it with chopped fresh dill and sliced avocados.
8. Your dish is ready to be served.

3.7 Icelandic Curried Haddock Recipe

Preparation Time: 10 minutes
Cooking Time: 30 minutes
Serving: 2

Ingredients:

- Jalapeno, a quarter cup
- Lemon juice, a quarter cup
- Red onion, two
- Lime juice, a quarter cup
- Fresh chopped cilantro, a quarter cup
- Haddock cubes, one pound
- Tortilla chips, as required
- Chopped tomatoes, two
- Chopped avocados, one cup
- Sesame seeds, as required
- Spicy red curry paste, two tablespoon

Instructions:

1. In a large boiling pot of water, add the shrimps.
2. Boil your tuna cubes and then drain them.
3. In a large bowl, add all the rest of the ingredients except the avocados.
4. Mix your ingredients and then add avocados in the end.

5. Add the cilantro on top.
6. Your dish is ready to be served.

3.8 Icelandic Fish Stew with Rye Bread and Lemon Recipe

Preparation Time: 10 minutes
Cooking Time: 40 minutes
Serving: 2

Ingredients:

- Fish broth, one cup
- Turmeric powder, one teaspoon
- Onion, one cup
- Lemon juice, half cup
- Fish cubes, half pound
- Lemon wedges, as required
- Powdered cumin, half tablespoon
- Smoked paprika, half teaspoon
- Water, one cup
- Minced garlic, two tablespoon
- Minced ginger, two tablespoon
- Cilantro, half cup
- Olive oil, two tablespoon
- Chopped tomatoes, one cup

Instructions:

1. Take a pan.
2. Add in the oil and onions.
3. Cook the onions until they become soft and fragrant.
4. Add in the chopped garlic and ginger.

5. Cook the mixture and add the tomatoes into it.
6. Add the spices and fish cubes.
7. Add in the broth.
8. Mix the ingredients carefully and cover your pan.
9. Add lemon wedges on top and serve it alongside rye bread.
10. Your dish is ready to be served.

3.9 Icelandic Salmon Soup Recipe

Preparation Time: 10 minutes
Cooking Time: 10 minutes
Serving: 4

Ingredients:

- Chopped white onions, one cup
- Chopped celery, one pound
- Potatoes, one cup
- Chicken stock, one quart
- Unsalted butter, three tablespoon
- Dried thyme, one teaspoon
- Minced garlic, one teaspoon
- Nutmeg, half teaspoon
- Heavy cream, one cup
- Tomato paste, one cup
- Salmon meat, one pound

Instructions:

1. In a large pan, add the chopped onions in the butter.

2. When soft and translucent, add in the minced garlic.
3. Add in the stock, thyme, salmon, nutmeg, potatoes and the celery leaves.
4. Add in all the rest of the ingredients and cook the ingredients until the salmon and potatoes are ready.
5. Cook the soup well for ten minutes and then check the soup.
6. If not thick, then cook your soup for an extra few minutes.
7. Your dish is ready to be served.

3.10 Icelandic Lobster Soup Recipe

Preparation Time: 10 minutes
Cooking Time: 10 minutes
Serving: 4

Ingredients:

- Chopped white onions, one cup
- Chopped celery, one pound
- Potatoes, one cup
- Chicken stock, one quart
- Unsalted butter, three tablespoon
- Dried thyme, one teaspoon
- Minced garlic, one teaspoon
- Nutmeg, half teaspoon
- Heavy cream, one cup
- Tomato paste, one cup
- Lobster meat, one pound

Instructions:

1. In a large pan, add the chopped onions in the butter.
2. When soft and translucent, add in the minced garlic.
3. Add in the stock, thyme, lobster, nutmeg, potatoes and the celery leaves.
4. Add in all the rest of the ingredients and cook the ingredients until the lobster and potatoes are ready.
5. Cook the soup well for ten minutes and then check your soup.
6. If not thick, then cook the soup for an extra few minutes.
7. Your dish is ready to be served.

3.11 Icelandic Shrimp Salad Recipe

Preparation Time: 10 minutes
Cooking Time: 10 minutes
Serving: 4

Ingredients:

- Cooked shrimps, one cup
- Shredded carrots, one cup
- Green onion, one cup
- Chopped red cabbage, a quarter cup
- Chopped green cabbage, a quarter cup
- Chopped tomatoes, half cup
- Balsamic vinegar, half cup
- Olive oil, half cup
- Chopped parsley, half cup
- Grated ginger, two tablespoon
- Lemon juice, two tablespoon

Instructions:

1. In a large bowl, add the balsamic vinegar, chopped parsley, grated ginger and lemon juice.
2. Mix the ingredients together and keep it aside.
3. In the next bowl, add in the rest of the ingredients and mix well.
4. Add the dressing formed above.
5. Mix your salad and dressing.
6. Your dish is ready to be served.

3.12 Icelandic Shrimp Sandwich Recipe

Preparation Time: 30 minutes
Cooking Time: 10 minutes
Serving: 4

Ingredients:

- Mayonnaise, two tablespoon
- Salad leaves, as required
- Cooked shrimps, half pound
- Lemon juice, three tablespoon
- Avocado slices, as required
- Fresh chopped dill, one tablespoon
- Bread slices, as required
- Sugar, one tablespoon

Instructions:

1. In a bowl, mix the mayonnaise, lemon juice and sugar until it forms a homogenous mixture.
2. Toast your bread slices.

3. Add the mayonnaise, lemon juice and sugar mixture on top of the slices.
4. Add the cooked shrimps.
5. Layer the avocado slices and then the fresh chopped dill on top.
6. Add the salad leaves.
7. Your dish is ready to be served.

3.13 Icelandic Caramelized Potatoes Recipe

Preparation Time: 10 minutes
Cooking Time: 20 minutes
Serving: 4

Ingredients:

- Fresh chopped dill, three tablespoon
- Salt, to taste
- Black pepper, to taste
- Butter, one tablespoon
- Capers, one tablespoon
- White vinegar, four tablespoon
- Potatoes, one pound
- Brown sugar, half cup
- Lemon juice, half cup
- Lemon zest, one teaspoon
- Sour cream, half cup

Instructions:

1. In a large bowl add the butter and potatoes.
2. Fry the potatoes and then add the capers, salt, black pepper lemon juice and lemon zest.
3. Then add the brown sugar and white vinegar.
4. Cook your dish and dry out your mixture.

5. Add the chopped fresh dill on top.
6. Add a little sour cream to garnish it.
7. Your dish is ready to be served.

3.14 Icelandic Lamb Stew Recipe

Preparation Time: 10 minutes
Cooking Time: 40 minutes
Serving: 2

Ingredients:

- Fish broth, one cup
- Turmeric powder, one teaspoon
- Onion, one cup
- Lemon juice, half cup
- Lamb cubes, half pound
- Lemon wedges, as required
- Powdered cumin, half tablespoon
- Smoked paprika, half teaspoon
- Water, one cup
- Minced garlic, two tablespoon
- Minced ginger, two tablespoon
- Cilantro, half cup
- Olive oil, two tablespoon
- Chopped tomatoes, one cup

Instructions:

1. Take a pan.
2. Add in the oil and onions.
3. Cook the onions until they become soft and fragrant.

4. Add in the chopped garlic and ginger.
5. Cook the mixture and add the tomatoes into it.
6. Add the spices and lamb cubes.
7. Add in the broth.
8. Mix the ingredients carefully and cover your pan.
9. Your dish is ready to be served.

3.15 Icelandic Hot Chocolate Recipe

Preparation Time: 10 minutes
Cooking Time: 10 minutes
Serving: 2

Ingredients:

- Unsweetened cocoa powder, four tablespoon
- Sea salt, a quarter teaspoon
- White sugar, two tablespoon
- Whole milk, two cups
- Vanilla extract, a quarter teaspoon
- Whipping cream, as required

Instructions:

1. Take a small pan.
2. Add in the milk and boil it.
3. Add in the vanilla extract, white sugar, sea salt and unsweetened cocoa powder into the milk.
4. Boil your hot chocolate until it becomes thick.
5. Add your hot chocolate into glasses.
6. Add the whipping cream on top.
7. Your dish is ready to be served.

3.16 Icelandic Sandwich Loaf Recipe

Preparation Time: 30 minutes
Cooking Time: 10 minutes
Serving: 4

Ingredients:

- Fresh chopped dill, three tablespoon
- Salt, to taste
- Black pepper, to taste
- English bread, as required
- Butter, one tablespoon
- Cucumber slices, as required
- Cooked shrimps, one pound
- Mayonnaise, half cup
- Cooked prawns, half pound
- Red bell pepper, two cups
- Hard boiled eggs, as required

Instructions:

1. Take the English bread and take it on a dish.
2. Spread the mayonnaise on top of the bread.
3. Layer the cooked shrimps and prawns.
4. Then the hard boiled eggs and red bell pepper.
5. Add the butter on top and then the cucumber slices.
6. Add salt and pepper on top and roll your sandwich.
7. Add fresh chopped dill on top.
8. Slice your sandwich.
9. Your dish is ready to be served.

3.17 Icelandic Creamy Langoustine Soup Recipe

Preparation Time: 10 minutes
Cooking Time: 10 minutes
Serving: 4

Ingredients:

- Chopped white onions, one cup
- Chopped celery, one pound
- Potatoes, one cup
- Chicken stock, one quart
- Unsalted butter, three tablespoon
- Dried thyme, one teaspoon
- Minced garlic, one teaspoon
- Nutmeg, half teaspoon
- Heavy cream, one cup
- Carrots, one cup
- Tomato paste, one cup
- Langoustines meat, one pound

Instructions:

1. In a large pan, add the chopped onions in the butter.
2. When soft and translucent, add in the minced garlic.
3. Add in the stock, thyme, langoustines, nutmeg, potatoes and the celery leaves.
4. Add in all the rest of the ingredients and cook the ingredients until the langoustines, carrots and potatoes are ready.
5. Cook the soup well for ten minutes and then check you soup.

6. If not thick the cook your soup for an extra few minutes.
7. Your dish is ready to be served.

3.18 Icelandic Grouse with Berry Sauce Recipe

Preparation Time: 30 minutes
Cooking Time: 10 minutes
Serving: 4

Ingredients:

- Olive oil two tablespoon
- Chicken stock, six cups
- Heavy cream, two cups
- Butter, two tablespoon
- Carrot, one
- Cornish game hens, four
- Dried blueberries, one and a half cup
- Dried thyme, one and a half teaspoon
- Salt, to taste
- Black pepper, to taste
- Fresh blueberries, one and a half cup
- Red wine vinegar, half cup
- Ginger, one teaspoon
- Green apple, one
- Cinnamon, two teaspoon

Instructions:

1. In a large pan add all the ingredients except the berries, cinnamon and red wine vinegar.
2. Cook your ingredients well for ten to fifteen minutes.

3. When your chicken is cooked, and dried properly, dish it out.
4. In a small sauce pan, add the berries, cinnamon and red wine vinegar.
5. Cook your mixture well.
6. The end result should be a thick berry sauce.
7. Add the mixture on top of your chicken.
8. Your dish is ready to be served.

3.19 Icelandic Cocoa Soup Recipe

Preparation Time: 30 minutes
Cooking Time: 10 minutes
Serving: 4

Ingredients:

- Potato starch, one tablespoon
- Water, two cups
- Milk, three cups
- Cocoa powder, three tablespoon
- Sugar, three tablespoon
- Cinnamon, half teaspoon
- Salt, a pinch

Instructions:
1. Take a pan and heat it well.
2. Add in the milk and let it boil until it froths.
3. Add in the cocoa powder, sugar and cinnamon into the boiling milk.
4. Low the heat down and cook your mixture.
5. Add in the water and salt into the mixture and cook for two minutes.
6. Add in the potato starch.

7. Cook your soup until it thickens.
8. You can add any cream as a topping on your soup if you like.
9. Your dish is ready to be served.

3.20 Icelandic Leaf Bread Recipe

Preparation Time: 30 minutes
Cooking Time: 10 minutes
Serving: 4

Ingredients:

- Cater sugar, one and a half teaspoon
- Whole milk, a quarter cup
- Vegetable oil, for frying
- Unsalted butter, two tablespoon
- Plain flour, to cups
- Salt, half teaspoon

Instructions:

1. Mix all the ingredients together to form a dough structure.
2. Make small round ball structures from the dough.
3. Make leave cuts with the help of a blade on the dough.
4. Fry your dough balls.
5. Dry them with a paper towel.
6. Your dish is ready to be served.

Chapter 4: The World of Ancient Viking Recipes

Following are some ancient Viking recipes that are rich in healthy nutrients and you can easily make them with the detailed instructions list in each recipe:

4.1 Sweet and Savory Viking Chicken Recipe

Preparation Time: 10 minutes
Cooking Time: 30 minutes
Serving: 4

Ingredients:

- Fresh chopped dill, three tablespoon
- Salt, to taste
- Black pepper, to taste
- Chicken drumsticks and thighs, one pound
- Brown sugar, two tablespoon
- Tomato sauce, one cup
- Chopped onion, one cup
- Minced garlic, one tablespoon
- Minced ginger, one teaspoon
- Green chili, a handful
- Lemon juice, two tablespoon
- Olive oil, three tablespoon
- Capers, one teaspoon
- Potatoes, two cups
- Chicken stock, one cup

Instructions:

1. Take a large pan and heat it properly.
2. Add the olive oil and onions into the pan.
3. Cook the onions until they turn translucent.
4. Add in the garlic and ginger paste.
5. Cook your mixture and add the spices into it.
6. Add the chicken thighs and drumsticks and cook your mixture properly coated it all over your chicken pieces.
7. Add the tomato paste and potatoes.
8. Simmer it and when the mixture dries out add in the stock, chili and capers.
9. Add brown sugar and lemon juice.
10. Cook your chicken and potatoes for ten to fifteen minutes.
11. Your dish is ready to be served.

4.2 Viking Brown Bread Recipe

Preparation Time: 30 minutes
Cooking Time: 10 minutes
Serving: 4

Ingredients:

- Caster sugar, one and a half teaspoon
- Whole milk, a quarter cup
- Brown sugar, one cup
- Baking powder, one teaspoon
- Unsalted butter, two tablespoon
- Whole wheat flour, one cup
- Plain flour, to cups
- Salt, half teaspoon

Instructions:

1. Mix your dry ingredients in a bowl.
2. Make sure you mix in the wet ingredients separately first and then add it into the dried mixture.
3. Make a dough structure from the mixture but the dough should not be very thick.
4. If the formed mixture is thick, add in more milk to gain the desired consistency.
5. Bake your bread by placing it in a baking dish that is greased properly.
6. Your brown bread may take hardly twenty minutes to bake.
7. Dish it out and slice it up.
8. Your dish is ready to be served.

4.3 Viking Flat Bread Recipe

Preparation Time: 30 minutes
Cooking Time: 10 minutes
Serving: 4

Ingredients:

- Wheat flour, three cups
- All-purpose flour, two cups
- Rolled oats, one cup
- Water, as required
- Baking soda, one tablespoon
- Salt, a pinch
- Milk, one cup

Instructions:

1. In a bowl add the dried ingredients well.
2. Mix the wet ingredients in a bowl first and then add it up into the wet ingredients.
3. Mix the dough and then knead it properly.
4. When the dough is completely kneaded form a round structure from it and place it on a baking tray.
5. Add some oats on top of the bread.
6. Bake your bread for about ten to twenty minutes.
7. When your bread will turn crispy from the outside dish it out on a rack.
8. Slice it up when it cools down.
9. Your dish is ready to be served.

4.4 Viking Green Soup Recipe

Preparation Time: 30 minutes
Cooking Time: 10 minutes
Serving: 4

Ingredients:

- Fresh chopped spinach, one cup
- White leeks (chopped), two cups
- Bouillon, two cups
- Black pepper, to taste
- Grated ginger, one teaspoon
- Nutmeg powder, half teaspoon
- Heavy cream, half cup
- Egg yolk, two
- Parsley, half cup

Instructions:

1. Wash and dry the spinach leaves.
2. Wash your white leeks and slice them up.
3. Boil your bouillon until it becomes tender.
4. Add the spinach and leeks into your bouillon.
5. Boil your dish for five minutes.
6. Add in the parsley and boil your dish a few minutes more.
7. Add in the salt, pepper and ginger into the dish and boil your mixture by covering it with a lid.
8. In a small bowl add the cream and egg yolks.
9. Mix the egg yolks properly into the cream to make a homogenized mixture.
10. Add the egg yolk and cream mixture into the soup.
11. Keep stirring the soup to avoid lump formation.
12. Add the nutmeg into the soup mixture.
13. You can place it alongside a bread slice if you want.
14. Your dish is ready to be served.

4.5 Viking Field Peas with Turnip Recipe

Preparation Time: 10 minutes
Cooking Time: 40 minutes
Serving: 4

Ingredients:

- Fresh chopped dill, three tablespoon
- Green peas, one pound
- Turnips, one pound
- Milk, four cups
- Wheat flour, two teaspoon
- Bacon, one cup

Instructions:

1. Take a large bowl.
2. Add the turnips into it.
3. Then add the wheat flour.
4. Add some water to mix it.
5. Add the milk at the same time.
6. Dissolve them well.
7. Then add the green peas and the bacon into it.
8. Add the spices if you want.
9. Cook it for twenty-five minutes.
10. Your dish is ready to be served.

4.6 Viking Crock Pot Stew Recipe

Preparation Time: 20 minutes
Cooking Time: 25 minutes
Serving: 2

Ingredients:

- Chopped onions, one cup
- Minced garlic, one teaspoon
- Minced ginger, one teaspoon
- Potatoes, two cups
- Sliced bacon, ten slices
- Cabbage (sliced), one
- Beer, one cup
- Water, one cup
- Smoked sausage, one cup
- Heavy cream, one cup
- Olive oil, two tablespoon

Instructions:

1. Take a large pan and heat it well.
2. Add the olive oil and onions.
3. Cook your onions until they become translucent.
4. Add in the garlic and ginger paste.
5. Add in the potatoes and smoked salmon.
6. Cook them properly and add a little water when the mixture dries up.
7. Add the cabbage once the above mixture is cooked properly.
8. Cook your mixture well and then add the water and beer.
9. Cook your mixture well.

10. In a separate small pan, add some olive oil and fry the bacon slices.
11. When the slices turn brown on both sides, dish them out
12. Let them cool down.
13. Add the heavy cream into the crockpot mixture.
14. Your mixture will start to thicken.
15. When it reaches your desired consistency dish it out.
16. Crumble the bacon slices on top.
17. You can garnish it with chopped cilantro or fresh chopped dill.
18. Your dish is ready to be served.

4.7 Viking Salmon with Flatbread Recipe

Preparation Time: 20 minutes
Cooking Time: 40 minutes
Serving: 3

Ingredients:

- Nuts, one cup
- Bread, five pieces
- Yogurt, one cup
- Eggs, five
- Mozzarella cheese, as required
- Mix spices, one tablespoon
- White sugar, one tablespoon
- Salmon filet (cut into small cubes), one pound

Instructions:

1. Take a large bowl.
2. Add the salmon pieces into it.
3. Add the nuts and the cheese.
4. Combine them well.
5. Then add the eggs and the salt.
6. Then add the yogurt and olive oil.
7. Add the sugar as required.
8. Mix all ingredients well.
9. Then bake it for half an hour.
10. Your dish is ready to be served.

4.8 Viking Nut Bread Recipe

Preparation Time: 10 minutes
Cooking Time: 30 minutes
Serving: 2

Ingredients:

- Nuts, one cup
- Bread, five pieces
- Yogurt, one cup
- Eggs, five
- Cheese, as required
- Spices, if you want
- Sugar, to taste

Instructions:

1. Take a large bowl.
2. Add the nuts and the cheese.
3. Combine them well.
4. Then add eggs and salt.
5. Then add the yogurt and olive oil.

6. Add the sugar as required.
7. Mix all ingredients well.
8. Then bake it for half hour.
9. Your dish is ready to be served.

4.9 Viking Steamed Mussels Recipe

Preparation Time: 10 minutes
Cooking Time: 35 minutes
Serving: 2

Ingredients:

- Mussels, half pound
- Heavy cream, one cup
- Salt, to taste
- Pepper, to taste
- Garlic powder, one tablespoon
- Saffron threads, two pinches
- Butter, half cup

Instructions:

1. Take a pan and add olive oil.
2. Add the mussel pieces into it.
3. Add the onions in it and fry them.
4. Add the heavy cream and mix them.
5. Add the salt and pepper as required.
6. Then add some water and mix ingredients again.
7. Add the saffron threads into the mixture.
8. Then cook it for thirty to thirty-five minutes.
9. Add the fresh chopped dill on top of your dish.
10. Your dish is ready to be served.

4.10 Vikings Stone Age Bread Recipe

Preparation Time: 10 minutes
Cooking Time: 40 minutes
Serving: 3

Ingredients:

- Raw almonds, half cup
- Walnuts, one cup
- Sunflower seeds, one cup
- Olive oil, half cup
- Eggs, five
- Plain whole wheat flour, two cups
- Kosher salt, one tablespoon

Instructions:

1. Take a large bowl.
2. Add the nuts and the seeds.
3. Combine them well.
4. Add the flour into the mixture.
5. Then add the eggs and salt.
6. Mix all ingredients well.
7. Add your mixture into a baking dish and add the olive oil on top.
8. Bake your bread for thirty to forty minutes.
9. Once brown color is attained on top of your bread and is completely cooked, dish it out on a rack.
10. Cut it up into slices.
11. Your dish is ready to be served.

4.11 Vikings Barley Porridge Recipe

Preparation Time: 6 minutes
Cooking Time: 30 minutes
Serving: 2

Ingredients:

- Whole barley, half cup
- Water, two cups
- Cinnamon, one or two
- Sugar, to taste

Instructions:

1. Soak the barley in two cup water.
2. Add three cups of water in saucepan.
3. Add the cinnamon and mix.
4. Then boil the water for few minutes.
5. Add the soaked barley into boiling water.
6. Add the sugar as required.
7. You can add the nuts and fruits in the end.
8. Your dish is ready to be served.

4.12 Vikings Rabbit Stew Recipe

Preparation Time: 20 minutes
Cooking Time: 40 minutes
Serving: 2

Ingredients:

- Fresh chopped dill, three tablespoon
- Salt, to taste
- Black pepper, to taste
- Rabbit meat, one pound
- Garlic powder, two tablespoon
- Ginger, one tablespoon
- Spices, as required

Instructions:

1. Take a pan and add olive oil.
2. Add the lamb meat pieces into it.
3. Add the onions in it and fry them.
4. Add the spices and mix them.
5. Add the salt and pepper as required.
6. Then add some water and mix the ingredients again.
7. Wash the vegetables properly and add them into the pan.
8. Cook your dish for thirty to fifty minutes.
9. Your dish is ready to be served.

4.13 Vikings Lamb Recipe

Preparation Time: 10 minutes
Cooking Time: 30 minutes
Serving: 4

Ingredients:

- Lamb meat, two pound
- Garlic powder, four tablespoon
- Yoghurt, one cup
- Ginger, five tablespoon
- Salt, to taste
- Black pepper, to taste
- Spices, as required

Instructions:

1. Take a pan and add the olive oil.
2. Add the onions in it and fry them.
3. Add the spices and mix them.
4. Add the salt and pepper as required.
5. Then add some water and mix the ingredients again.
6. Wash the meat properly and add in the pan.
7. Cook your dish for thirty to fifty minutes.
8. Your dish is ready to be served.

4.14 Vikings Lamb with Mint and Garlic Recipe

Preparation Time: 30 minutes
Cooking Time: 50 minutes
Serving: 4

Ingredients:

- Lamb, one pound
- Mint, one cup
- Garlic powder, two tablespoon
- Ginger, one tablespoon
- Spices, as required
- Salt, to taste
- Pepper, to taste

Instructions:

1. Take a pan and add the olive oil.
2. Add the lamb meat into it.
3. Add the onions in it and fry them.
4. Add the spices and mix them.
5. Add the salt and pepper as required.
6. Then add some water and mix the ingredients again.
7. Wash the mint properly and add in the pan.
8. Cook your mixture for thirty to fifty minutes.
9. Your dish is ready to be served.

4.15 Vikings Apples and Bacon Recipe

Preparation Time: 10 minutes
Cooking Time: 30 minutes
Serving: 4

Ingredients:

- Bacon meat, one pound
- Chopped onions, two
- Apples, two
- Cloves, a few
- Spices, as required
- Salt, to taste
- Black pepper, to taste

Instructions:

1. Cut the bacon into pieces.
2. Fry them on medium heat.
3. Add the butter and the onions.
4. Add all the spices and mix all the ingredients.
5. Heat it until it becomes soft and slight brownish.
6. Your dish is ready to be served.

4.16 Vikings Honey Roasted Chicken Recipe

Preparation Time: 30 minutes
Cooking Time: 50 minutes
Serving: 6

Ingredients:

- Butter, two tablespoon
- Chicken, two pounds

- Ginger, one tablespoon
- Chopped tarragon, two
- Honey, one tablespoon
- Salt, to taste
- Black pepper, to taste

Instructions:

1. Take a dish and add the chicken in it.
2. Then add salt, pepper and mixed herbs.
3. Rub the chicken with all ingredients.
4. Melt the butter and honey in a separate pan.
5. Bake for thirty minutes.
6. Turn the chicken upside down and bake for additional twenty minutes.
7. Your dish is ready to be served.

4.17 Vikings Chicken Stew with Beer Recipe

Preparation Time: 10 minutes
Cooking Time: 30 minutes
Serving: 2

Ingredients:

- Yellow onions, three
- Chicken, one pound
- Diced carrots, three
- Dark beer, one bottle
- Salt, to taste
- Black pepper, to taste
- Thyme, one tablespoon
- Garlic powder, two tablespoon
- Ginger, one tablespoon

Instructions:

1. Cut the chicken into small pieces.
2. Cut the carrots into pieces.
3. Fry the chicken in butter for five minutes.
4. Add the salt and pepper to taste.
5. Then add the carrots, garlic powder and ginger.
6. Add thyme and mix all ingredients.
7. Then boil the mixture for fifteen minutes.
8. Cook until the vegetables become tender.
9. Your dish is ready to be served.

Conclusion

Our everyday life rotates around our bustling timetables and discovering something beneficial to eat turns out to be a low priority, particularly for people who work vivaciously. In such conditions, health is compromised to a greater extent, which can cause many side effects in the future. To avoid such conditions, it is very important to eat healthy and eat right.

Combined with heavy emphasis on wellbeing and ethical developmental philosophy, the Nordic Cuisine platform has a creative approach to conventional foods. Nordic cuisine, nationally and globally, will build and encourage the pleasure of cooking, flavor, and variety. Nordic dishes are typically simple, and seafood, potatoes, meat, and berries being used in many traditional meals. Fresh, raw ingredients that can be found in abundance or that come freshly from the seas are the basis of most Nordic cuisine.

Nordic cuisine is straightforward, and this is called husmanskost-the farmer's fare. It is normal and genuine, made with the land's staple product. There is no reason to over-complicate things when you deal with the finest produce of Nordic cuisine. This book covers the life of a Scandavian, making it easy for them to prepare their favourite recipes inside their kitchen without any stress. Being a Scandavian is not difficult with all these amazing and easy to make Swedish recipes, Norwegian recipes, Icelandic recipes and recipes of ancient Vikings.

www.ingramcontent.com/pod-product-compliance
Ingram Content Group UK Ltd.
Pitfield, Milton Keynes, MK11 3LW, UK
UKHW021923190726
13853UKWH00002B/810